In Memory of

James (Jim) Nading

by

Family and friends.

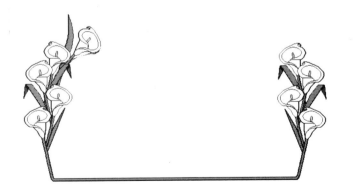

H is for Hawkeye

An Iowa Alphabet

Written by Patricia A. Pierce and Illustrated by Bruce Langton

Text Copyright © 2003 Patricia A. Pierce
Illustration Copyright © 2003 Bruce Langton

Sleeping Bear Press
310 North Main Street, Suite 300
Chelsea, MI 48118
www.sleepingbearpress.com

Sleeping Bear Press is an imprint of The Gale Group, Inc.,
a division of Thomson Learning, Inc.

Printed and bound in Canada.

10 9 8 7 6 5 4 3 2 1

Library of Congress Cataloging-in-Publication Data
Pierce, Patricia A., 1967-
H is for Hawkeye : an Iowa alphabet / by Patricia A. Pierce ; illustrated
by Bruce Langton.
p. cm.
Summary: The letters of the alphabet are represented by words, set in
short rhymes with additional information, relating to the state of Iowa.
ISBN 1-58536-114-3
1. Iowa-Juvenile literature. 2. English language-Alphabet-Juvenile literature.
[1. Iowa. 2. Alphabet.] I. Langton, Bruce, ill. II. Title.
F621.3 .P54 2003
977.7—dc22   2003013141

*To John—may we continue to grow in faith and love
and to Jared and Andrew, our blessings.*

*My gratitude to my parents, Greg and Darlene Origer,
and to Terry Libbey, Cherie Danduran, Mary Wagner,
and A Way With Words—your support and
encouragement is truly appreciated.*

*Special thanks to Heather Hughes and
Amy Lennex of Sleeping Bear Press.*

PATRICIA

*This book is for all the children that I met through my
school presentations…Best of luck to all of them in the future.*

*My thanks to Sleeping Bear Press and
Patricia A. Pierce for all their hard work to
make another great project come to life.*

*My love for my family goes without saying.
Rebecca, Brett, and Rory…you are the best.*

BRUCE

Artist Grant Wood was born on a farm near Anamosa and is known for his paintings of Iowa's landscape and people. His famous masterpiece, *American Gothic*, can be viewed at the Art Institute of Chicago.

American Gothic portrays a farmer and his unmarried daughter posing in front of their house. The simple Gothic window of the house influenced the title of the painting. The American Gothic House, located in Eldon, is listed on the National Register of Historic Places.

A a
A

A is for *American Gothic*,
a famous painting by Grant Wood.
He painted a picture of a farmer and his daughter,
in the barnyard they stood.

1903-1931

Leon Bix Beiderbecke

Leon Bix Beiderbecke was born in Davenport and is one of America's most original and accomplished jazz musicians. Bix was a cornetist, pianist, and composer and was known for his use of harmonies in jazz.

The Quad-City Times Bix 7 began in 1975 with fewer than 100 runners and has grown into one of the premier running events in the country. The Junior Bix 7 was added in 1998 for children 12 years old and younger.

B is for Bix Beiderbecke,
his music has pizzazz!
Swing your hips and clap your hands
as we dance to his jazz.

B b

Carrie Chapman Catt
is our letter **C**.
Women receiving the right to vote
was a great victory.

Carrie Chapman Catt

Carrie Chapman Catt, leading women's suffrage advocate, was raised in Charles City and graduated from Iowa State University. She was a teacher and principal in Mason City and became one of the nation's first female school superintendents. She was also a member of the Iowa Woman Suffrage Association.

Carrie played an important role in women winning the right to vote. She was a respected and admired speaker. Under her leadership, the National American Woman Suffrage Association gained the support of the U.S. House and Senate. In 1920, the 19th Amendment was passed and women were granted the right to vote.

Iowa became the 29th state on December 28, 1846. Iowa's first capitol building was located in Iowa City. In 1857 it was decided to move the state capital to a more central location in the state. Des Moines was chosen as the new capital city. Des Moines was originally a military outpost. Iowa's government rules under the golden dome, which is gilded in 23-carat gold.

Des Moines is home to Terrace Hill, an historical Victorian-style mansion. Terrace Hill has been home for Iowa's governor and family since 1972.

Des Moines is the largest city in Iowa and a center for the insurance business. It is also a major manufacturing city.

D is for Des Moines,
the capital with the golden dome.
It's the place where laws are made
and our governor's home.

E is for Eastern Goldfinch,
with feathers of yellow, white, and black.
Thistle and sunflower seeds
are its favorite snack.

Iowa's state bird is the Eastern Goldfinch and is commonly found throughout the state. During the summer, male goldfinches are bright yellow with a black cap and black tail and wing feathers marked with white feathers. Female goldfinches do not have the black cap and are a lighter yellow color. Eastern Goldfinches usually remain in Iowa during the winter and both the male and female birds' feathers turn a brownish color. They nest late in the summer when thistle and sunflower seeds are available.

Many early developments of 4-H began in Iowa. School superintendents, such as O.H. Benson and Cap E. Miller, and teachers such as Jessie Field Schambaugh played important roles in establishing 4-H Clubs.

The idea of using a clover to represent the 4-H youth development program began in 1906 at the Goldenrod School in Clarinda, when Superintendent Benson was visiting the one-room county school. Students gave Superintendent Benson four-leaf clovers they had found at recess. The four H's on the clover represent Head, Heart, Hands, and Health.

Dyersville is home of the *Field of Dreams* movie site. The movie was based on the book *Shoeless Joe*, by William P. Kinsella. He studied at the Iowa Writers' Workshop at the University of Iowa.

Ff

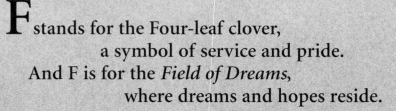

F stands for the Four-leaf clover,
a symbol of service and pride.
And F is for the *Field of Dreams*,
where dreams and hopes reside.

The geode is the official state rock of Iowa. A geode is a hollowed-out stone formation with a sparkling lining of mineral crystals.

The Grotto of the Redemption is a religious structure located in West Bend. Father Paul Dobberstein started construction on the Grotto in 1912. Besides containing geodes, the Grotto displays rocks from every state. It is the largest man-made collection of minerals, gems, stones, coral, ores, fossils, and petrified wood in any single place on Earth. The Grotto was registered as a National Historic Landmark on February 23, 2001.

Gg

Our state rock, the Geode,
begins with the letter G.
Many sparkling Geodes
in the Grotto you will see.

GEODE

GROTTO

H h

H is for Hawkeye,
the nickname of our state,
given to honor Chief Black Hawk,
a leader brave and great.

Iowa's nickname, the Hawkeye State, is believed to be a tribute to Chief Black Hawk of the Sauk tribe. His Native American name was Black Sparrow Hawk.

Chief Black Hawk disputed a land agreement and fought to retain land that belonged to his ancestors. He was defeated in a battle known as the Black Hawk War in 1832.

CHIEF
BLACK HAWK

Iowa State Fair

I is for the Iowa State Fair,
with blue ribbons for first place.
Rides and shows will make you laugh
and put a smile upon your face.

The Iowa State Fair, located in Des Moines, is one of Iowa's largest events and tourist attractions. The fair is well-known for its competitive livestock judging, craft and art shows, amusement rides, grandstand entertainment, demonstrations, and contests. In 1941 a cornstalk measuring 23 feet and 2 and ½ inches tall won the National Tall Corn Contest.

The Iowa State Fair was the inspiration for the novel *State Fair* by Phil Stong, three motion pictures, and a Rodgers and Hammerstein Broadway musical.

The Iowa State Fair is also known for Norma "Duffy" Lyon's famous life-size butter-sculptured cow. It takes Duffy approximately 20 hours to create the cow out of an estimated 550 pounds of butter.

J j

J is for a movie star;
John Wayne was his name.
Acting like a cowboy
gave him worldwide fame.

John Wayne, whose real name was Marion Michael Morrison, was born in Winterset. Also known as "The Duke," John Wayne is remembered for his roles as a tough, idealistic cowboy.

His restored childhood home in Winterset is now a museum with rare photographs of John Wayne and props from his movies, such as the eye patch worn in *True Grit* and a suitcase used in *Stagecoach*.

JOHN WAYNE

One tiny kernel of corn grows into a corn stalk eight to ten feet tall, with each ear of corn containing 500 to 1,000 kernels! Equally amazing, each ear of corn always has an even number of rows. There are usually 14 or 16 rows with about 40 to 50 kernels in each row.

From 1920 to 1930 farmers would enter their best ears of corn in county fairs and festivals to be judged on the uniformity and shape of the kernels. As a youth, Henry A. Wallace, who was born in Adair County and later served as our 33rd Vice-President of the United States, questioned the idea that the best-looking corn was the best-yielding corn. As a student at Iowa State University, he did research on corn yield and genetics. He developed a high-yielding hybrid and founded Pioneer Hi-Bred International Seed Company. The production of hybrid seed corn is a major Iowa industry.

K is for the Kernels on the corncob.
Let's shell them one by one.
We'll pop out every kernel
by using our big thumb.

Oh, this is so much fun!

L is for Livestock—
chicken, sheep, cattle, and hogs.
You can find them in the barnyard
along with two playful dogs.

L1

Iowa is one of the top-producing livestock states in the nation. Iowa ranks first in hog production. Beef and dairy cattle also play a significant role. Iowa ranks among the leading milk-producing states, with most of the milk used for making butter, cream, and powdered milk. Sheep and poultry are also produced on many farms.

Frederick Louis Maytag began his business career by manufacturing farm implements in Newton, Iowa. In 1907 he developed a wooden washtub in an effort to offset the seasonal slumps in business. The washing machines became so popular that Maytag focused the attention of his company on the production of washing machines. Today the Maytag Corporation is a leading manufacturer of home and commercial appliances, floor care products, and vending machines.

M is for Mr. Maytag
and his washing machine.
Spin cycle! Rinse cycle!
Now your clothes are clean.

N is for the Native people
of the past and of today.
Celebrate at a powwow—
come sing, dance, and play.

Sacred Native American burial mounds are found in the Effigy Mounds National Monument in northeastern Iowa. The mounds are believed to be 2,500 years old. Many of the mounds are effigies—burial mounds built by Native Americans in the shape of birds and animals.

Approximately 17 different Native American tribes resided in Iowa. Iowa is named after the Iowa River, which was once the site of large villages of the Iowa (pronounced Ioway) tribe.

In 1846 the U.S. government relocated the Meskwaki people to Kansas. Unhappy with this relocation, the Meskwaki raised money by selling their horses and purchased land along the Iowa River. The lands are a settlement rather than a reservation. The Meskwaki Powwow celebrates and preserves their heritage.

Joway

Sioux

Sauk

O is for the Oak,
   our official state tree.
Look carefully among the leaves,
   and acorns you will see!

Iowa has never specified what kind of oak is its official state tree, but the state's most common oaks are the white oak and the bur oak. Oaks are deciduous trees, which means that they shed their leaves in the fall. The fruit of the oak is the acorn. Many birds and animals such as deer, pheasants, quail, squirrels, and chipmunks depend on acorns as an important part of their food source.

The branches of an oak tree provide shelter for many birds and animals and its hard, strong wood is used in making furniture and flooring.

O o

Herbert Hoover was the 31st president of the United States. His birthplace in West Branch is a National Historic Landmark. The Herbert Hoover Library was dedicated in 1962 and contains a vast collection of the president's memorabilia.

Before serving as president, Herbert Hoover was a successful mining engineer and began public service by organizing and supervising the distribution of food relief programs that saved many thousands of lives. During Herbert Hoover's term as president, the United States faced the Great Depression after the stock market crashed. He was the first president to use the power of the government to fight a depression and did not accept a salary. He gave all his income to charity and to public service projects.

P is for President Hoover, elected in 1928.
Do you have dreams of becoming the next president from our state?

31st

1929-1933

Herbert Hoover

Q q

The Quaker Oats Company is our letter Q.
Making snacks and cereal is what they like to do.

The Quaker Oats Company was formed in 1901 when a cereal mill in Cedar Rapids operated by John and Robert Stuart and George Douglas joined with two milling companies from Ohio. Besides being a top producer of cereal, The Quaker Oats Company produces other food products such as sport beverages, syrups, grain-based snacks, pasta, and rice products. The Quaker Oats Company is known as a symbol of quality, purity, and honesty.

Iowa is bordered on two sides by navigable rivers. The Missouri River flows along Iowa's western border and the Mississippi River forms its eastern border.

One of the largest and longest touring bicycle events in the world begins and ends at Iowa's bordering rivers. Two Des Moines newspaper columnists started an annual bicycle ride across the state of Iowa in 1973. The ride begins along Iowa's western border, where riders can dip the back tire of their bicycle into the Missouri River. The ride ends along Iowa's eastern border, so riders can complete the ride by dipping their tire into the Mississippi River.

Rr

Cruise down a River
for the letter R.
Travel the Missouri and Mississippi
in a boat, not a car!

S s

S is for the Seal,
a symbol of our state.
It shows many reasons
why our state is great.

The Great Seal of Iowa represents Iowa's agriculture and industry. Iowa's motto, "Our liberties we prize, and our rights we will maintain," is displayed on the streamer held by an eagle. The governor uses the seal for official documents and the seal can only be used with the governor's permission.

The state motto can also be found on Iowa's flag. Iowa became the 29th state on December 28, 1846, but didn't officially adopt a flag until 75 years later. After the Civil War it was felt the only flag necessary was our national flag. The action to create a flag was taken during World War I when Iowa National Guardsmen suggested a state flag was needed to designate their unit.

The blue stripe on Iowa's flag represents loyalty, justice, and truth. The white stripe is for purity, and the red stripe stands for courage.

John Froelich built the first gasoline tractor in 1892 and helped form the Waterloo Gasoline Traction Engine Company. This one-cylinder tractor was an operating success and was able to move forward and in reverse.

In 1918 John Deere purchased the Waterloo Company and tractors became an important part of the John Deere Company.

T is for Tractor
that runs like a deer.
To inventor Mr. Froelich,
let's give a cheer!

Iowa has three state universities
for the letter U.
Which one to go to
will be up to you.

Iowa takes pride in its educational system and has three state universities. The University of Iowa, Iowa City, was Iowa's first public institution of higher learning, founded in 1847 and known worldwide for its Writers' Workshop. The Old State Capitol building is part of the University of Iowa's campus.

Iowa State University in Ames is among the nation's leading universities in research accomplishments. George Washington Carver, noted plant scientist, received his education from Iowa State University. The first electronic digital computer was invented at Iowa State University by John Atanasoff and Clifford Berry.

The University of Northern Iowa, Cedar Falls, was founded in 1876 to train teachers for the state's public schools.

Uu

Seven charming Villages
are for the letter **V**.
Let's go for a visit—
pack your bags and come with me.

The Amana Colonies consist of seven villages that were founded in the mid-1800s by a religious group of German craft workers and scholars. In 1965 the Amana Colonies were designated as a National Historic Landmark with over 475 historic buildings and sites. The peace and charm of the quaint villages and their fine arts and crafts have made them one of Iowa's leading tourist attractions.

Iowa's state flower, the wild rose, has five petals and blooms in shades of pink. The Iowa General Assembly designated the wild rose as the state flower in 1897. It was chosen as an Iowa symbol because it decorated the silver table service Iowans presented to the battleship USS *Iowa*.

W is for Iowa's state flower,
the delicate Wild rose.
Try to find it in the tall prairie grass
as the wind gently blows.

X x

The letter **X** is found in Sioux City,
    where a monument stands tall.
Sergeant Floyd's service to America
    we honor and recall.

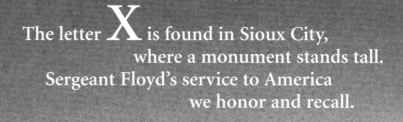

Clark

Lewis

Siou X City

The Sergeant Charles Floyd Monument in Sioux City is the first historic landmark registered by the United States government. The 100-foot-tall monument marks the burial place of Sergeant Floyd, the only fatality of the Lewis and Clark Expedition. The site overlooks the beautiful Missouri River and offers an excellent view of Sioux City.

Y y

Y Where the tall corn grows,
stands for Yield.
Crops grow in the rich soil
covering the farmer's fields.

Iowa ranks first among the states in corn production and is often referred to as the land where the tall corn grows. The majority of the corn is fed to live-stock, but the rest is ground into powder or soaked in liquids to create by-prod-ucts that are used in making a variety of food and industrial products. Iowa is also a leading producer of popcorn.

The fertile, rich, black soil of Iowa makes the state one of the country's leading crop production states. Iowa yields huge quantities of corn, soybeans, oats, hay, wheat, and barley. Soybeans are Iowa's second most valuable crop. The soybean and oil extracted from it are also used in a wide range of food and industrial products.